RAFAELLA
MACHADO

ATELIÊ FASHION

gorgeous patterns to color

GALLERY BOOKS

New York   London   Toronto   Sydney   New Delhi

G

Gallery Books
An Imprint of Simon & Schuster, Inc.
1230 Avenue of the Americas
New York, NY 10020

First Gallery Books trade paperback edition January 2017

GALLERY BOOKS and colophon are registered trademarks of Simon & Schuster, Inc.

For information about special discounts for bulk purchases,
please contact Simon & Schuster Special Sales at 1-866-506-1949
or business@simonandschuster.com.

The Simon & Schuster Speakers Bureau can bring authors to your live event. For more information or to book an event,
contact the Simon & Schuster Speakers Bureau at 1-866-248-3049 or visit our website at www.simonspeakers.com.

Manufactured in the United States of America

10   9   8   7   6   5   4   3   2   1

ISBN 978-1-5011-6178-0

for Marcela Filizola,
for teaching me that the only error is to never take risks

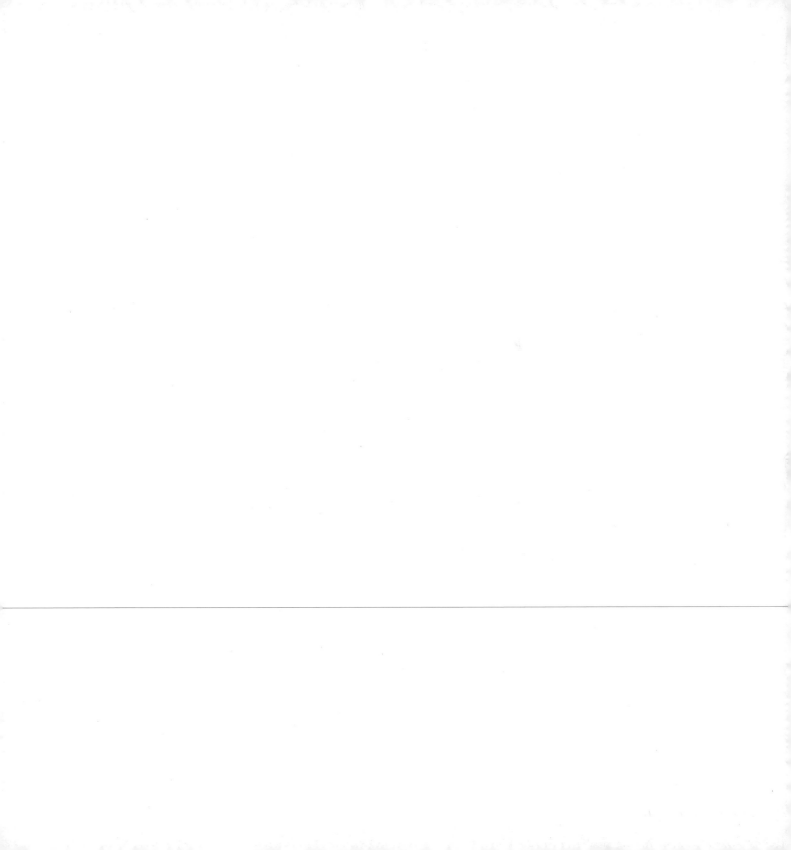

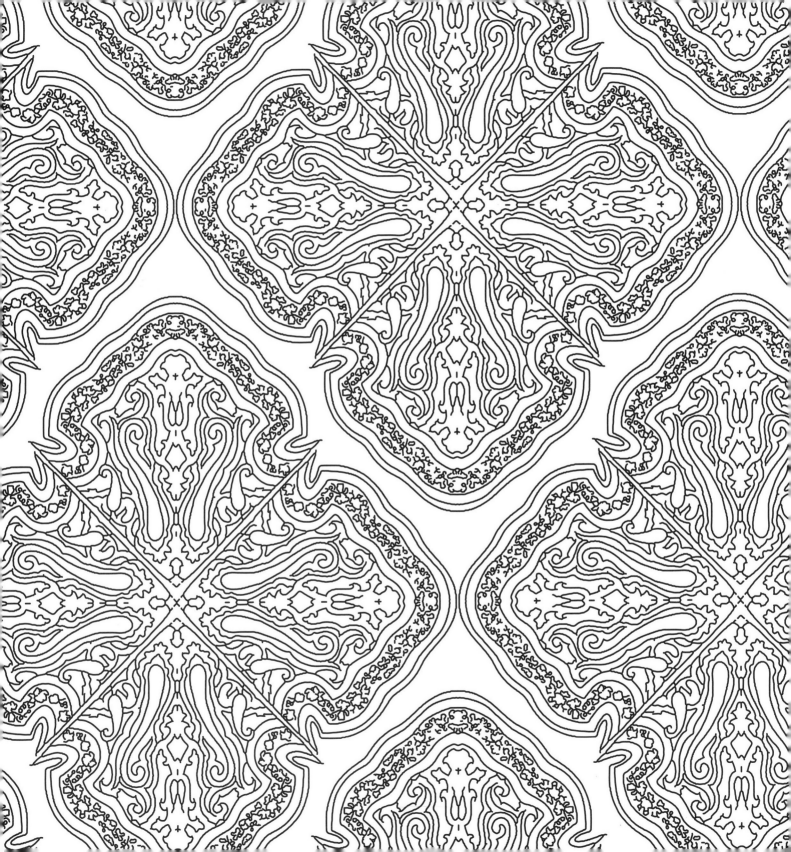

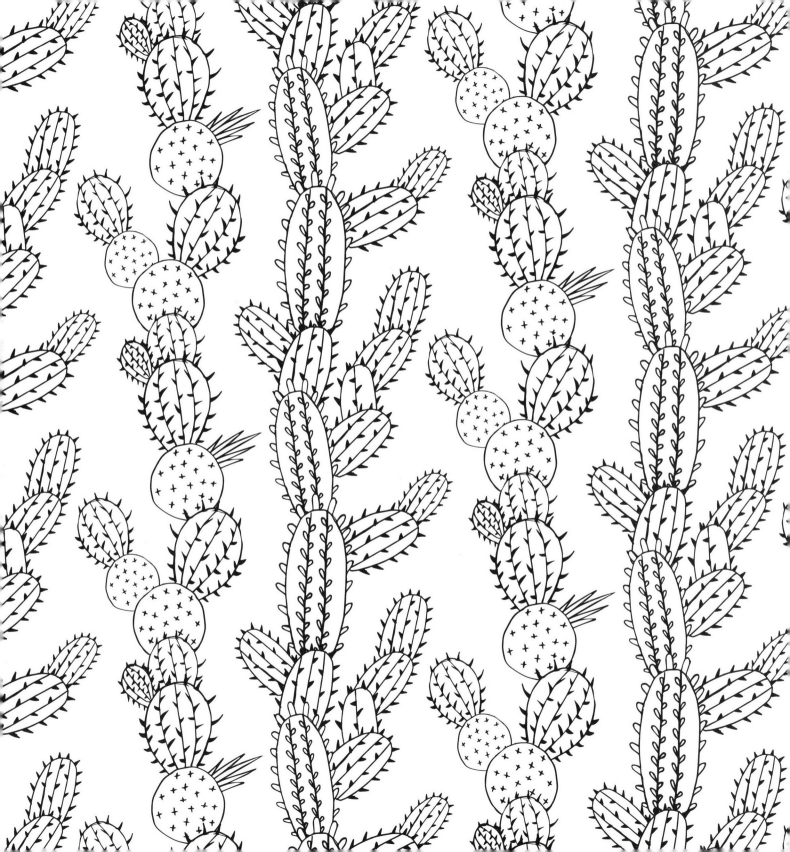

Acknowledgments

I would like to thank my family for making this book possible. My parents and sisters, Roberta and Izabella, for supporting me always. The team at Galera, which is my second family: Ana Lima, Adriana Hidalgo, and Paula di Carvalho. Also all the employees at Group Editorial Record, and Victor Monetegro, Estefania Zaramella, and Fernanda Bonvini, for teaching me so much about design.

To my dear friends: Marcela, Tatiana, Leonardo, Paula, Mari, Victor, James, Fernanda, and many others who do not fit here.

Thanks for everything—without you, life would not be fun.

Rafaella Machado studied design at PUC-Rio and specializes in surface design at the New York School of Visual Arts. She has since developed patterns for various products such as wallpapers, fabrics, and stationery. Her passion for patterns comes from the belief that all that is good is worth repeating. She shares an apartment in Leblon with two cats, Sofia and Lola.